AF241645

The Emotional Handbook

plus

A Thankful Season

Tedd

Table of Contents

Table of Contents

A Thankful Season

Dedication

The Emotional Handbook

I want to dedicate this book to my love
and to my therapist. Without the both
of you this book would not be a reality.
If you have mental health issues,
please seek help. End the stigma. There
is no shame in asking for help.

A Thankful Season

Both of these books would not be if it
weren't for the helpful staff at KRCC.
Because of them I reached my goal
of stability n happiness. I'm forever
grateful.

The
Emotional Handbook

By

Tedd

Daily Journal

I've set in motion my emotional
journey
Rediscovering my emotions
The good, the bad, the indifferent
I've setup my daily journal
To keep track of my days
Just the basics
Just give people my compass
As to where I am on this journey
It feels weird to start this journey
I'm not sure I'm ready for this
But are we ever ready for it
Isn't that the point of this journey
To start with one step n take
another
I guess the end goal would be
recovery
To be living not just surviving
For we've been on survival mode
For too long...

First step

Taking this first step
I guess you'll call it nervous
I'm unsettled on where this day
Will take me
But I'm giving myself the
permission
To feel what ever feeling comes to
me
Let it be what it is
I haven't written in awhile
I'm not sure how to take this
journey
I'm not sure what words to use
Can I do justice to this journey
Will it be for not
But here I am taking me first
step...

The ABC's of emotions

I guess I should start with the
Basics of emotions
What is it that I'm feeling
How does it make me feel
How does it effect my physically
I guess I need to separate it
Down from just
Negative or positive but get to the
meat
Of the emotion
If it's positive is it joy, happiness,
euphoric
If it's negative is it depress,
sadness,
Anger
I've been numb for so long not
feeling
Anything
I've been so overwhelmed that I
haven't
Allowed myself the option to feel
I've been dumping, suppressing,
sweeping

Under the rug
For so long my hoard of emotions
Has become a monster
Now I guess I got to wrestle the
monster
I got to get my head out of the
sand
N give myself a chance to feel my
emotions
Be true to them n let me be what
They are…

Epic Love Story

Is it wrong of me to want an epic
Love story
The kind that's in legends n movies
Where one day I meet the guy
Of my dreams
N fall madly in love
To give all of me to him
To let my guard down
N open my heart to the possibility
Of an epic
Unconditional love story
Am I emotionally ready for that
Kind of love
Do I have that kind of love in me
I've been so cut off from the world
Would I even realize that someone
Has come
Into my life just for that purpose
To be my epic love story…

The Monster in my Mind

What started out as a simple
Coping mechanism
Has become a monster in my mind
The trauma of my youth
Was too much to deal with
N I had no one to talk to
I had no one to tell me how to deal
With the stuff
That I did a data dump
I didn't allow myself to remember it
I suppressed it
Put it in a box n buried it
Now it's become this monster
Where now I don't remember
anything
Good or bad
It's almost like dementia
I could even tell what I did 5
minutes ago
Plus on top of that my sense of
reality
Is so screwed up

I'm not even sure what's real or
not
So I have two things controlling me
How do you fight them
How do you overcome them
It would be nice to actually
Remember something
Not just have it be a ghost…

Simple Words

It's been so long since I've allowed
myself
To be creative
I'm not sure if I still have it in me
Can I find the right words
Can I allow myself to go to the
places
That I've hidden for so long
Can I be vulnerable enough
Can I expose the inner workings of
My mind n heart
Can I do it justice
Am I going to be able to be
That raw again
To allow myself to delve into
These emotions
Can it still be authentic
Can it be from the heart
Can it bring you in n make you think
n feel
Will my words be too simple…

Home

It would be nice to finally
Have a home
Not just a physical one
I guess an emotional one as well
A safe harbor
Someplace where I can thrive
Someplace where I can place my
roots
N know they will grow n produce
fruit
Or at least flowers
I want to see the beauty within n
outside
To feel safe enough to delve
Into this emotional journey
It would be nice to have a place of
my own
One where I feel like I can
maintain it
Be it mine n not have to share it
unless

I want to
To have it be on my terms
N not the terms of others
It be nice to finally say this is
home…

Man of my dreams

If I could create the perfect man
for me what would he be
I know I like tattoos n a nice
bubble butt
I like a nice mix of meat n muscle A
solid build
But he needs to be more than
physical
He needs a heart to love like a
Two way street
To see my short comings n be ok
with them
To be my rock so that I may soar
Among the clouds
To dream the dreams that only
Dreamers dream
Yet know that I can also be his rock
that
I'll be there for him
My dream lover would be
affectionate
That when it's the right place n
time

To show me affection
To want to hold me, kiss me, n love
me
Comfort me that would be so nice to
finally
Have a shoulder to cry on n know he
will be
There to comfort me
To let me know it's ok
It's ok to cry or smile or laugh
Or fall apart
Cuz he will be there
Knowing when it's his turn I'll do
the same It will be nice to have
the man of my
dreams…

Numb

Cut off
Turned off
Removed from within
Not allowing them out
Not giving them their moment
Not giving them shape or form
Not giving permission to feel
To be numb
Inside n out
To be void of anything
Other than the noise
The constant voices n thoughts
The madness of the mind n soul
To be nothing other than numb…

Thoughts n voices

To be bombarded
A constant stream
Of thoughts n voices
Till it's to a point
Where I can't tell them apart
I can't tell what's real or not
I've lost touch of reality
I have no support system
To say what is real or not
Where the illusion begins n ends
It's just this constant white noise
That I'm constantly trying to
cancel out
It's exhausting
It takes up all of my energy
It takes all of my being
I'm lost to it's overwhelming
nature
It's nothing but thoughts n
voices…

Role model

Is my simple life enough
Are my trails n trauma deep enough
Are my wounds big enough scars
that
You can see n touch
Can someone learn from my
mistakes
Can someone see the light at the
end
Of this life
Can I be a role model
To show that you can survive this
That there is more than just
survival
That it's ok one day all this would
Be for something
That the meaning will be revealed
That you too can have your moment
In the sun
N bask in it's warmth
How can I say
What could I say to make a
difference

Is my voice steady enough
Can the actions of one person really
make
A difference in someone else's life
Have I come to the point in my life
Where I can turn to someone
N say you got this…

Admission of flaws

Ok time to face the firing squad
Flaws

Impulsive
To the point I spend money when
I know I shouldn't
To the point I don't make logical
choices

Addictive
To the point where I play too many
Phone games that
It's beyond a coping skill

Suppressive
To the point where I no longer
remember
Things
To the point it's destructive
o the point where I'm numb to
emotions

Nonsupportive
to the point where I have cut
myself
Off from others
To the point where I should ask for
Help n don't
To the point where I no longer
speak with
Friends n family

Abusive
To the point where I lash out
N hurt others
To the point I've hurt myself so
bad
I no longer
See the good inside
Despite this my one strength of
survival
Has kept me alive n I could me
more
Cold n jaded
Yet I have stayed warm once I let
My guard down

N open myself to the possibilities that

Are in front of me...

Hidden tears

Underneath the glossy exterior
Is a river of tears
Inside of me I shed tears
Of loneliness n heartbreak
I do not let them out for fear
That they will never stop
If I cried on the outside people would
See my weakness
N toss me away for not being stronger
The scar of being told to only
Show happiness
Has been with me my whole life
To the point where it's become an excuse
Excuse to not allow myself the opportunity
To cry other than watching a movie
It's sad that I can let go of this scar
hat all my tears are hidden tears...
A manual

Maybe there is n I am unaware of
it
Yet why is there not a manual to
emotions
Like step one if you feel blank then
Do action
A manual that's if your are
physically
Feeling this
N your heart says this
N your mind is say the following
then your
Emotion is blank
If feeling blank emotion then seek
out help
Or share with closest friend or
family
Or enjoy that emotion cherish it
protect it
A manual on how we can force
ourselves out
Of the negative emotions
Be able to say just do the following
n you'll
Be good as rain

But at lass such a manual probably
Wouldn't work
Each person feels emotions
differently
Each person see their emotions
uniquely
I think emotions are like people
No carbon copies
No two snowflakes are the same
But a manual to life would be nice to
have…

Building Bridges

I've burnt so many bridges in my
life
I lost count
Now here I am recovering trying to
piece
My life back together
How do I build bridges
How do I reach out
Where do I start from
What's the first step
Do I apologize for past indiscretions
Do I put all my cards on the table
Reveal all
What do I do at this point
This is all unfamiliar
This is places n spaces
I've never thought I'd be in
I don't have a blue print
I actually don't even have a clue
As to how to build bridges…

Heartfelt Joy

For once in my life I feel heartfelt
joy
I hear the music in my heart
My mind sings along
My toes are tapping
I actually hear the birds singing
The sun glistening on my face
My whole body feels warm
I could dance like no one there or
business
The overwhelming delight
Can't be contained
I just want to shout out in joy
Grab someone's hand n let them
know
That they are loved
And share this heartfelt joy…

Grateful Beginning

I guess I should be grateful
I know I don't have much
But I should be grateful for
The small things
I do have
I'm thankful for having a place
To live that also
Provides me meals to eat it's one
less thing
To worry about
I'm thankful for my phone it gives
me the
Ability to stay
In communication with the world
I'm thankful for my health I'm
still alive
I'm thankful for the ability to
Write in words
How I feel n being able to make
sense I know I don't have much
stuff but I'm thankful
For what little I have

I'm glad I have somewhere to
have
Grateful beginning…

Puddles

It sucks staying inside while it
rains
But there is one thing I love
About the rain
Is puddles
I can play n stomp in them
I can reflect on them
I can splash in them
I can sweep them away
With puddles
Is a seed of childhood of days gone
by
When we don't have a care
Where life is uncomplicated
I want to be that kid again
Enjoying the puddles…

The Future

I know we're not supposed to worry
About the future
But I hope we are allowed to
dream about
I wish in the future that I have a
home
I have someone special to cherish
A group of friends to enjoy
I hope the future comes
N it's the life I've always dream
about
I hope that as bad as the past
N present are
Is how good the future is
That I can dream a million dreams
Color in all of the rainbow
Shine like I was the only star in
The night sky
I hope the future
Is all of that n all of the stuff I
can't
Even begin to dream of…

Tides of hurricanes

Whirling n twisting
Destroying n creating
Rolling in n out like the tides of the
ocean
Blowing strong
Hollering like a steam train racing
Down the tracks
Created from the warm waters of
Anger n addiction
Hurricanes of life come n go
Like the seasons
They are unpredictable yet they
follow
Patterns of behavior from
Past experiences
They affect all around n no one is
safe
But like all things they past
We pick up the pieces of our lives
Keep the parts worth saving
Letting go the parts that no
Longer benefit us

And make preparations for the next one…

A night out

The thumping beat calls to my
Animal instincts
The thirst for lust calls to my inner
demons
Slowly I twist n turn
Moving my hips drawing in my prey
Like the Borg resistance is futile
I have sex on the table n
I have a full deck
I play my cards like a hustler
Making them think they are winning
Yet the black widow in my heart
Waits patiently knowing when to
strike
Silly games we play on a night out
Like tonight…

The lotus of my heart

The lotus flower has been
represented
In so many ways
Yet I find myself drawn to it's form
I've used it to represent
The Lord, the Son n the Holy Spirit
I've used it to represent
My past, future, present
With it's many colors
It's delicate pedals and beauty
It's softness in the world
I can think of a better symbol
To represent my heart n soul…

Peaceful

I step onto the natural path
Worn down by others, animals, rain
I smell the wild flowers blooming
See the moss covered rocks
I hear the calm breeze rustle the
leaves
In the trees
I feel the warmth of the sun's
rays
Upon my skin
I take each step slowly
Allowing myself to bask in the glory
That surrounds me
Slowly I breathe in n out
Allowing myself to let go all of my
stress
Calmly I slow my thoughts n focus
In on all the beauty of nature's
glory
Each step lightly touching the
ground
Like I'm walking on a bed of clouds

I pause to take a picture of the
path
So that I can remind myself
What peaceful is…

Nightmares come at dusk

As I slip in n out of conscious
Not sure if I'm really awake or in a
dream
The scary monsters start creeping
In the shadows of my mind
I can feel my spine tingling
Each hair stands up
Ants crawling on my skin
My breath quickens
My senses alert waiting in
anticipation
The fear grips me do I run do I
fight
I hear the footsteps in the distant
Are they following me
The panic envelopes me making
My mind race
With thoughts of blood
Then suddenly the thrust of the
knife
His arm around me not letting
Me get away

His breath on the back of my neck
Thrust another stab
I begin to go lifeless
I cut off my physical self
My mind wanders to a different
place
The coldness brings to cover me
My senses begin to go numb
There I lay naked in the night
Dawn comes ashame sets in
The hidden secret I must bear
To young to know what to do
To guilty to ask for help
The crime goes unsaid for years to
come
Dusk comes the nightmares come
out
To play again…

Finger snap

Snap
It cuts the air
Get over here

Fills the room
The taste n smell of alcohol
On my lips

Snap
Echoes in my mind
Time for your duty
The panic rushes over me
How am going to do this

Snap
Like lightning in the night
Get over here
Again thunders in the room
Lord give me the strength
Enters my mind

Snap

I can still hear them today
I still cringe n shiver
But then the days of love
Cover the wounds
The days filled with laughter
The fur babies we shared
The brief moments
Where you were not a mean drunk

The days where your words
Were not abusive but gentle
And kind
A love that still haunts me till
this day…

One third

It started so innocently
Let's try sharing each other with a
third Let's enjoy the moment with
another
Then became you couldn't be with
me
Unless it was with another
Soon I my value diminished
Soon I was removed from the
equation
Soon it was late night outs
I'm over at a friend's house
I still remember seeing you with
him
N you trying to deny any wrong
doing
Then the emails to the secret lover
Saying how I couldn't give you up
The freedom I felt the day the
door closed

Behind me knowing I was just one
third
Of you
But one whole of me…

To my former true love

I was so young n naïve
Didn't yet know the ways of the
heart I'm sorry I have forgotten
your name
Your now just a ghost in my memory
But I remember the night of bliss
I remember feeling like there was
No other man like you
I remember telling you I would stay
That I would give up my dreams
for you
Yet you let me go
You gave me the opportunity
To see life
If I had one wish
It would to be with you again
I wonder from time to time
If your life turned out ok
Were you loved did life treat you
right
There are times I wished I had
stayed
N not listen to you but

Would regret fill my heart
N turn to bitterness
Would I have been the same as
I am today
Yes bad things happened
But from them I grew strong
Gave me the courage to see the
world
Courage to write n be published
Yet you linger
A question never to be answered
Of what would have been…

Hello my dear

The dawn has come I wrestle
From my slumber
Slowly opening my eyes
As the sun awakens the room
There you are still asleep
The look of peace over your face
Slowly your eyes open
You turn towards me morning love
Whispers from my lips
I gently stoke your face
I go in for a kiss
Welcome to a new day
A day we get to spend together
Each day is a new day
A new chance to make sure
We get it right
N then you say I love you
N my heart melts
I'll cherish each morning like this
Here with you…

Moving Day

It's moving day the movers have
arrived
This old shack is about to be torn
down
Time to say goodbye
You spent time weeding thru the
hoards
You boxed everything
Separated the stuff going to
The new home
From the stuff going to the thrift
store
N the stuff going in the trash
You made peace with the shack
Yes there was good memories
Yes there were bad but the lessons
Learned will carry with you
The shack will always hold a pass
In your heart
But at last it's time to move on
Your new home is one that dreamt
about

One that prayed for
And in it you will thrive…

It's ok mom

Mom I have nothing but love for
you
But it's ok
Ok to move on from the past
And finally let it rest
Ok to see the positive
Ok to rebel n buck the system
Ok to laugh, cry and smile
It's ok for me to finally
Move on with my life
If that means leave you behind
Then that's what I need to do
I can no longer be that child in your
head
It's ok if you never see all the
adventures
All of the dreams and
All of the achievements

It's ok

I finally understand it is not about
you
It's about me
I have already forgiven you
Now I need to let you go…

Land of opportunity

I think I've found someone
I hope it's real n not a figure
Of my imagination
He has seen my flaws n ok with
them
He sees my dreams n believes in
them
He sees my heart n knows its true
I may stumble
I may fall but it's been a while
Since I've been here
It's been a while since we let
someone in
It's been a while since we
Let ourselves love
But now we are in the land of
opportunity
Where we go who knows
What may come is unknown
But I welcome it all with open arms
And I relish in the idea that
I have someone
To take this journey with...

Call of the west

The call of the untamed wilderness
Beats in my heart
To be one with nature
To see the stars n swim in them
To see the animals n the awe
Of the beauty
It's not a wise choice
It's a risk but one all the same
I should make
I've been safe I've put family first
Now I need to put me first
And my love
If he hears the call of the west
Then I should also answer
It's siren call
And let my heart be free…

Do ya speaka my language

Each culture has its own unique
language
Code words inside jokes
But what is my language
I'm a northerner in the south
But I've lived all over
I'm spiritual but not religious
I'm gay but don't follow the same
beliefs
I'm a poet but don't follow the
rules of
English
So what is my language
Is it words of the heart n soul
Am I multilingual
Who are my people
What is my culture
I've lived alone or been alone most
Of my life
I haven't had the luxury of friends
And community
I've just bounced around blending in
Observing those around me

Being a mirror image of what they
wanted
Am I a trailblazer
Am I before my time…

What does pride mean

It's gay pride month
I'm supposed to celebrate
The accomplishments
I'm supposed to celebrate the
history
I'm supposed to celebrate the
freedoms
But to be honest I really don't
follow
The gay community

I know we now have marriage
I know we are making strides in
adopting
I know we can now serve openingly
I know we longer hide in closets
I know we no longer marrying
women
For the sake of appearance
For me personally
I see a different view
We still not always able to get
services

At homeless shelters n get
attacked
We have to hide our gayness
I know churches still see us
Vile evil humans
Who only live in sin n have no part in
God's plan
I know that people scam us
For those brave
Enough to look for love with just
one person

I've never really got into the
Whole bar scene
I only went for the music n dancing
I've been judged time n time again
For not meeting the standards
Of being gay
Like too fat or not fat enough
Not butch enough not from enough
Not financially stable enough
I've never been enough
I like men but that seems
To be the extent

Of my relationship with the gay
community
That seems to be our only bond...

Wild horses

They can not be tamed
They are wild
They love the feel of the wind in
their hair
The way their feet touch the
ground
They hear call n answer it
Even if you try to ride them
They only let you for so long
N it's because they let you
Not because you roped them
They are majestic
Roam the wild spaces
Smell the flowers
See the beauty
Their hearts beats with passion n
fury
Nothing can stop
The stampede of wild horses...

Crack open the door

I have cracked open the door
I did it slowly cuz I knew if not
I would be overwhelmed with
emotions
But I have let out n brought
In some fresh air
To the musty depths of my mind
I've allowed myself to be ok
With the ghosts of memories past
I've allowed myself to feel them
Experience them let them go
Some things will be treasured
Some things will probably be forgot
again Some things I will make
peace with
I know that these ghost are part
of me
I must accept them
I know that I must keep the
Door cracked open
That what's done is done
It's time to move on...

Gravesite

I'm dreading it, this day of all days
The day I have to visit
The day I have to endure Get in
the car drive
The whole time trying to think of
What to say, what to do
How do make peace
How do you say your sorry
You saw the signs n ignored them
You thought you had more time
You thought this will pass
You saw him fading into the mirror
Now all you can do
Is on this day
Visit his site n say goodbye…

Tired of being alone

I wish life came with a manual
Step by step guide
On how to make n keep friends
How to fall in love
How not to get hurt
I'm tired on being a one man island
I wish for more than anything
Is a friend right now
Someone who I can share
This life with
See movies, go camping n hiking
Cook for, laugh with
Cry on their shoulder n know I'm
safe
I would be super excited if it was
More than one but I'll settle for
one
For now at least I wouldn't be alone
I have someone's back n they
Would have mind
Just wish I wasn't alone anymore...
Dancing

I forgot how much fun it is
I forgot how much a workout it is
I forgot what I was like
Hear the music pulsating Feel the
beat
My heart beats in time with it
My feet glide on the floor
My hands waving in the air
Feeling sexy even though I know
I'm way too fat but I'm getting
My groove on
Shaking my body twisting n turning
Forgetting all the troubles
Forgetting all the cares
N just dancing…

Without knowing it

I started therapy to deal
With the trauma of the past
All long I thought I've been
hoarding
My feelings n emotions
And I thought I was burying all
the pain
But I think somewhere
Inside of me was processing
Was taking all the stuff n
organizing
Cuz I thought it would be this
Huge overwhelming wave of stuff
But it hasn't been
Maybe I made peace with it
Without knowing I was
Maybe this image of a house
Busting at the seams isn't
accurate
Maybe the past is waiting
Patiently for me to let go
Like an old friend at the train
station

Waiting at the platform
For the train to leave
So they can wave goodbye
And let the train take me
To my new life…

My new life

So here I am
I'm sitting in my new apartment
It ain't much I don't have any
furniture
I don't have much more than
clothes
N food
I don't have phone service
So for once in a long time
I'm actually cut off from the world
So here I am the start of a new
chapter
Got a home
Got a possible love in my life
Now all I need to do is figure out
How the story is going to go
Will the love turn out to be a scam
Or will he be the hero of the story
Do I need a hero
Can I be my own hero
Can I be no longer the victim
But the thriver

the one Who stands up n boldly says
I am here!
This is exciting I've never been
here
Before like this yes I've started
new
Chapters before but never
Have I been the hero
Never have I been ready to move
Forward n let go of the past
These steps are all new
Can't wait to see how the story
goes...

Sunset

The vacation is over
But what fun we had
Now we ride the clouds home
The sun sets
Our time will fade into memories
The drinks
The food
The islands
The stuff animals
N let's not forget Bingo
But as we fly home
I will make sure not to let this
memory
Fade into darkness
I will cherish the memory with
fondness
Two friends celebrating life...

Paradise

The warmth of the tropical breeze
The sun coming thru the trees
The smell of flowers fills the air
The cold drinks by the oceanside
The day just slowly goes by
The sound of gentle waves on the
beach
The crystal blue waters calling
Out my name
The troubles of home long
forgotten
Only being in the present matters
I could get lost here in paradise…

Days at the beach

Why do we wait till we are on
vacation
To live life
Go to the beach
Have a drink or two
Let the day pass without a care
In the world
Why can't we bring the beach home
With us but I guess that it is why
It's a vacation it's a special
moment
In time where we can be young
Let our hair down
And just spend our days at the
beach…

Glitz n Glamour

All the glitters may not be gold
But at sea all the glitters is
glamour At night
The ship comes to life at night
The dresses the tuxes
The people dancing to melodic beat
Songs of our youth just seem
To belong here at sea
The make us young n carefree
Where else can you live out your
fantasies
But at sea
Here on the ship home doesn't
matter
The job, the bills, the fights,
All the stress n worries just melt
away
Into nights of glitz n glamour…

Can't you hear it

The smell of the ocean air
The taste of the alcohol in the
fruity drink
The feel of the warm sand
Between your toes
Hear the music fill the air
See the blue waters gently waving
at you
Oh the sweet call of paradise
It's time to return to her
N be intoxicated by her siren song...

The day has arrived

After months of planning
After months of saving money The
day is here
Your at the port the ship is there
The passengers from the previous
voyage
Make their way home
But for you today is the day
We are going to celebrate our
birthday
We are going to celebrate life
We are going to party like there
Is no tomorrow
The ship is ours
The voyage is about to embark
I can't wait for what's in store…

My forever

I don't know why you chose me
I'm not very much
But you chose me
N say my forever
I hope I am your forever
I hope I get a forever
Of love n understanding
I hope I get a forever to
Get things right n to do right by
you
I hope I get a forever
Of laughter n tears of joy
I hope you mean it
Cuz I want a forever with you…

Summer tears

On a warm summer's day
The rain rolls in with the clouds
It looks like mist over the trees
Like the world is on fire
So is my heart on fire with love
It burns so bright that tears
Fall from my face
Some are tears of joy
Some tears of fear
Is someone as lowly as me
Worthy enough of your love
I worry someday the rose tint
Will fade from your eyes
N you'll see the person I am
Not the person you would like to see
Is that person going to be enough
So as the rain falls
So do the tears upon my face…

I hear the music

Each day I tune into the radio
Songs of love songs of heartache
Songs of memories
Each one I can almost see in my
mind
Some are from memory
Some are from imagination
Some I wish I was the girl
They were singing about
Some you are the girl
I wish I could sing about
Unfortunately there are not
Too many love songs about men
Loving men but that's ok
The feeling they invoke
Are the same
The heart skips a beat
The feet go tapping
And I badly sing along
Totally offkey
But the feelings are the same
The joy I feel when I think of you…

The unspoken words

Well I did it
I finally said the unspoken words
Was I too harsh
Did I get my point across
Well you hear them
Well you change
It took all the courage I had to
say them
Now that they are said
I'm worried
Will it hurt too much to hear them
I probably should have
Rehearse them went thru it a
couple
Of times to get them right
But now what was said is said
The words no longer unspoken…

Endings

My first book had a clear ending
My second was a collection
So the ending a little more less clear
My third book ever time I thought
Ok this the end something would
Pop up and a new ending appeared
This book circling back to my first
Book n touching on emotional
Issues but like my last book
The ending not so clear
My first book there was a clear
beginning
Middle n end
This one like third it's wandering
Curving
Taking it's time
I'm not sure of the journey
Do I just make and end
N say this it last call for alcohol
It's 2am time to go home
This emotional journey
It's just that a journey

So who's to say I can't end the book
And come back for a visit on the
next one
So where are we on an ending…

A Thankful Season

By

Tedd

Thank you

To all the lovers
There are too many to remember
But you helped me discover
The side of me that came naturally
The side of me I didn't want to
admit existed

To all the friends
Most only lasted a season
Most are now ghosts of my past
Yet you reminded me I'm not an
island

To all the of those
Who were there when I needed
Someone from stopping me from
taking
My life
You hold a special place in my heart

To my family
I know we are blood
I know we don't see eye to eye

I know we don't speak
Yet you are reminders
Reminders that we all come from
somewhere

To all of you I say

Thank you

All the seasons
All the twists n turns
If anything was different
I would not be the strong
Man I am today
I would not change a thing
Other than writing more
Poems so I had a better memory
Of your names n the wonderful
Things you've done

Thank you…

The bridge

I look back now n see how
This one moment
Short n brief
Changed everything

To this moment

Life was ignorant n bliss

After this moment
Life is ongoing struggle

There I was
At the bridge
Struggling with faith n life
I started a journey
Now I was about to end it

Sitting at the edge of the bridge
Staring at the vastness
Below
Lost

Then you said do you need a ride

A stranger
Someone who probably had
Better things to do
Stopped
Not just stopped to ask me
If I needed a ride
But also stopped me from
Doing something stupid
Which I think he knew

We talked during the ride
I thanked him for the ride
In the end
He gave me some money
And said that place can help
And from there the journey
Has continued
The journey is still not over
But I will always remember

The bridge n
Your kindness…

Struggling

I thought I closed the last season
I thought I was ready
For a new chapter

But I guess there was another
season
To go thru

I've been struggling
With finding my spark
With finding motivation
With finding me
Who am I anymore
Beyond my mental illness

Mental illness has complete
Control of my life

I've lost me
Am I anything more than
The sum of my highs n lows

I take my meds

I seek therapy

I try to stay stable

What else is there to me
Beyond this

Yes I have my poetry
N my creativeness
I can dream a million dreams
And still dream a million more
Yet none ever come true

I long to find a partner
Yet I never go anywhere
I gave up on online dating
It's nothing more than scams
Yet how do I find someone
In the middle of nowhere

I'm unhappy with my weight
I bought the videos
Yet can't seem to find the will
To do them

I seem to be stuck in life
I want change
I want a new chapter

Yet where's my spark
Where's my inner desire
I seem to be struggling
Struggling on how
To move on…

Forrest God

I know it's silly
It's just a drawing on a screen
But
He so hot

It's a drawing of a forest god

Reminds me a lot of me
There are days I wish I wake up
N be him

Reddish brown hair
Short on the sides
With just enough on top to run
Through but not too long

Arms big n strong

Chest just enough definition
But not too much

And the perfect chest hair amount

Which goes to the perfect

Stomach
A little meat on the sides
Flat without out rippling
N fur too

The rest I have to imagine
But I'm sure it's perfect too

Well maybe one day
I'll wake up
Go to the mirror
N be pleasantly surprised

N see I'm him…

What sexual

Demisexual

Asexual

Homosexual

Sex, sex, sex

Can we please start with emotions
Can we please start with a
connection
Can we please look beyond
All the physical attributes

Can we please
Just maybe
Start with hello

Hello, I'm Tedd…

Where's my Chris Pine

I know there's a debate
About the Chris's of the world
And yes there is an argument
For Chris Evans
When he is hairy n rugged
But people want him clean shave
N goody two shoes
Not me

But back to Chris Pine
He the perfect mix of bad boy
N good boy
His hair short on sides
N enough on top
He is good shaved or beard
He strong n athletic
Without being overly
Muscular
He comes across as kind n gentle
Yet there's that sense could
Be wild n fun in bed

He comfortable in his own skin
I'm sorry but out of the
Chris's

He the one
Just wish he had a gay twin
Who was unknown
N just a regular guy
On the street

I wish I could find
My version of him
Where I'd be good
Enough to date him…

Let's have some fun

Let's play in the puddles
Let's play on the beach
Let's play in bed
Let's have some fun

Dance to our own music
Paint with a million colors
Sing offkey n loudly

Let's have some fun

We can do it alone
Or in a group
Do it in the middle of the night
Or in broad daylight
But

Let's just have some fun...

What would the new chapter look like

I guess I never stopped
To actually think about
What is the new chapter

I'm going to be 50
I got maybe 25 good years left
If that
Most men die in my family by 75
So maybe I got 15 20 years
How do I want to spend these
years

I planned cruises
But how many more I can take
Not sure
Do I want to spend the rest of my
life
Here in this apartment
Where do I want to call home

Then there's can I keep being
single
I'm kinda over the single life

I'd rather share a life with
someone
Not so much to complete me
More share the journey with
Make memories
Have someone for the goals
N the days where I'm lost
And sad
To be connected to emotionally
Physically, n sexually

What will this new chapter bring…

Home

This subject has been in all
Of my books
It's the one thing I struggle with
I know it's supposed to be
Internal
N not actually a physical building
N yes
I should work on my internal home

Yet I also want a physical home too
Either of my own design
Or designed by someone
I want to walk into my home
N have it be a reflection of me

That is more than a house but
Home

Mine to cherish
Mine to show off
Mine to say this is me…

Keys

I know we spend a lot of time
On labels
Black, white, latin, straight, gay
Religious, non-religious
Old, young, male, female
N so on like we are
Pieces of clothing
Versace
Gucci

Which label is the best
Which labels quality over the rest

Why

Why *do* we have to live by labels

We are all made of the same flesh
We all bleed the same blood
We all are the same

Yet in this we are different but not
cus of physical things but personal
ones

Some of us long to be teachers,
Athletes, artists, writers
Some of us have desire to lead
Some like me struggle with
emotions

What truly makes us unique

Is our personality
The physical stuff is just the
dressing

In us our keys
They unlock doors in others
You might have what I need to
become the next person to walk on
Mars

Or paint the ninth wonder in the
world

We all have stuff lessons, ideas,
experience
Things you might not realize that
someone
Else needs

If we were more willing to put our
labels
Aside
Maybe we could see these keys
better
So see the person inside
N not just the limits of the labels…

Church

Here's my two cents
Sorry but churches are supposed to
be sheppards
They were not meant n not created
to be
Judge n jury

Churches were never meant
to create laws

The only judge is the Lord

The Lord
Does not hate
He only shows unconditional love
We are all his creations

He knows us before we are even
born
If he truly didn't want something
in the world
Then he would have never let it be
created

We are here which means he
created all of us
N loves each n every one

Churches should stop being the
judges
Start bringing the Lord's people to
him
And not push us all away from him

If it's truly end times
We need churches to bring us in
N not drive us to the Devil

Be an example of God's love
Show us how that even with our
flaws
There is beauty n light
In God's mirror…

The path

This has been the most difficult
path
My whole life it's always been a
struggle

World of man vs world of God

Straight vs Gay

Right vs Wrong

God vs Devil

The path the grey area with
either side fighting for my soul
I tend to choose the light
But have strayed in the dark

I've been searching for others
Whom I fit in with but never
Found my place
I always seem to be the outsider
Looking in

A Thankful Season

It's been a lonely path
I guess it was meant to keep me
strong n focused
But it would be nice
To find a rest area
Get a breather
Refill my battery

Maybe someday I'll find
My niche
But for now I'll keep to the
Path…

Today's grateful

Ok so back to topic
What am I grateful n thankful for

My neighbors
They have given me food n things
I've needed

Food n water
I have what I need to stay alive

My apartment
Even though I'd rather be in a
tent
In the woods
Yes it is nice to have shelter

My mom n Paul
They keep me sane

Mike
He came thru when I needed
Someone to fix my problems

My health
Other than being over weight
I got good health
I'm sure there's more but now
thanks...

The Blue Zen

The warmth of the Caribbean sea
With the sounds n smells of an Asian
temple
Where the heart basks
N the mind finds peace

The crystal blue waters gently
caress
The sands have you sink in
The sun shines melts the chills
Of the heart

The bowls hum n vibrate calming
All the racing thoughts

The chimes dance in the calm winds
Taking with it all the concerns

And finally the oms have you
Drift away to peaceful sleep
The Blue Zen
Where you become one...

The garden

It was barren
Just dirt
But visions of pink, purple n green
Came playing in my mind
So I decided to take a chance
And plant the garden

Where do you start

A fence
First I made a fence
Nice beautiful wooden fence
About hip high
This would define the garden

A path
A meandering path
To take you around
So the garden would reveal itself
slowly
This would divide the garden

A water feature
This would be the sounds
Of calmness n invite all living
Things to come enjoying
The garden
This would decorate the garden

A tree
This provide relief
To bring shade n the flowers grow
under it
This would defend the garden

ow to plant the flowers

Once complete
The garden will be ready to be loved
And my heart complete with it…

The perfect kiss

There he is
He comes to my door
I go outside
He says something
But I'm lost in his eyes

Gently
I place my left hand in his cheek
While my right hand presses
His chest
I close my eyes
As I go in
Our lips touch
Softly gently passionately

We kiss

I feel him get weak in the knees
N slide my right hand
Around his waist
To catch him
We are lost in the kiss

The world disappears

The galaxy ignites

We keep kissing

He slowly wraps his arms
Around me
Pulling us even closer
My left hand keeps
Caressing his cheek
My right hand pulling
Us close

This moment seems to go on
Forever
We kiss like we've been
Kissing for a thousand years

Lost in the kiss

Suddenly someone breaks
Our moment

I softly say if I never
Get to kiss you again
Then at least I have this one

Perfect kiss

Then I wake…

One more

It's just one more
Step

It's just one more
Second

It's just one more

I know the rain is loud
N the thunder deafening
N the wind beating you
To a pulp

But it's just one more

I know you can't see it
You are right there on the verge
The sunny days are on the other
edge
Of this storm it just takes

One more…

Sunny days

Funny how a year ago
I would have never thought
I'd have sunny days

Yet here I am
Basking in the sun
Smiling, laughing, excited
For the next chapter

It was the little things
Seeing my doctor
Talking to my therapist
Going to group therapy
Learning about my illness
N taking my meds

The thing that made the biggest
Difference was someone
Validating me

Telling my feelings
N my request for help

Was not unreasonable
Before I knew it
The sun arrived
And here I am happy
Truly happy for the first time in
my life…

Motivation

I know we are stuck in a routine
From time to time

I know we all giving in
N give up to this illness

But I ask you to find the courage
N the motivation
To keep going

There is no shame in saying
I can't handle this
N need help

If the first person can't help
Keep asking till you get the one
Who can

Trust me there is someone out
there
Waiting to help you
Sometimes it's their job

N sometimes it's cuz they care
N want to

I know it's hard to believe
But there is someone out there
Counting on you
N loving you…

My dream plan

If money were no problem
N I had enough of it
I would retire to the beaches
Of San Juan
Spend my winters
Basking in the sun drenched
Beaches
With gentle waves
Then when summer came
N the wild storms came rolling in
I leave for the safety
Of the state side
Live in a city that was just
One flight away
Yes that's my idea of heaven
On earth
That would be my dream plan…

Wonder n magic

The awe of kids
The simple joy kids are
They see what adults
Are too jaded to see
They believe in the magic
Where Santa Claus comes
N elf's roam the earth
Where gnomes
N fairies play their games
I try too hold on to my childhood
But I know it's slipping away
With each day I can feel
The magic n wonder fade
Ah to be a kid again…

Longing

I do admit
Long for another
To feel their touch upon my skin
The softness of their lips
To gaze upon their eyes
N forevermore swim in them
To be with another
To talk about everything yet
Say nothing at all
To share wonderous adventures
To see the world n the galaxies
Around us yet never leave
The couch
I long for my special person…

Work

Am I ready for the grinds of
Everyday living
To get up n get ready n go to
Work everyday
Am I ready to be on
N be the best version of me
Am I ready to be happy
N fake happy all day
To smile in the face of anger
Laugh with all the stress
I think I am
I feel more confident
Now that I got to feel
Real happiness n have sunny days
Even when it's raining outside
I think I can safely say
Bring it work…

Artsy poem

Romance
>> Becomes
>>>> Passion

Passion
>> Becomes
>>>> Desire

Desire
>> Becomes
>>>> Lust

Two lovers
>> Becomes
>>>> One heart of love

The stages of love
The steps two people go thru
Until the heart awakens
N all bets are off
The pattern of love are also
The madness of emotions

A Thankful Season

We look beyond the others
Shortcomings n only see
What the heart wants
N the body desires
Till either the end of time
Or the end of a season
When winter comes n chills
The flames n one must move on…

The emotional roommate

I now realize my mental
Illness
Is an emotional roommate
He has been unruly
For years now
Completely controlling
The house
But finally after some time
And patience
Understanding them

I now live in peace
With them
I finally can have friends
Over
N go for a walk
Without them

They no longer
Control the house

I have taken over

It's my house
They just living in it
Yes they still can be
Unruly
Yes they can still
Be noisy

But at the end of the day
It's my house…

Inspirational peer

Yes I think I'm ready
Ready to get in front
Stand up
N say you can be like me
You can have sunny days
You can have permission
To be silly, sad, happy
The whole gambit
Of emotions
I think I can inspire
Someone to not give up
Or give in

I think I can be a peer
Be a role model
N say this can be you too...

Whatever comes, comes

Whatever tomorrow
Brings
Winning the lottery
Getting a part time job
Being a peer support

Whatever it is

I'm ready
I have a full tool box
I have good meds
I have emotional support
I have a foundation

So tomorrow

Bring it

Happy, sad whatever
Comes, comes…

Ok I know that last poem was the
perfect ending to the book but here is one
last poem

Stages of rain with people

Person one
Runs from the rain
They see the storm clouds
They hear the thunder
N pack their bags n head for the
hills
To them life is an endless bowl of
strawberries n whip cream
All sun all time all happy
This is unrealistic
To have rainbows
You need rain

Person two
Ignores the rain
To them life is sitting in the house
cuddling on the couch n watching our
favorite movies

They won't admit to or see the
mountain of garbage
That is piling up in the house from
all the take out
They simply want to be
Blissfully ignorant
Of the rain

Person three
Lost in the rain
This person only sees rain
They don't see the helping hands
they don't see the sunny days
coming
It's all rain all days
They simply given up
Or have chosen to simply live in the
rain
This person I pray for n hope one
day they see all the help n sunny
days
That surrounds them

Person four
Hasn't dealt with rain
This person likes playing
In the rain n is making the best of
a bad situation
They have a rain coat n umbrella
they have the tools but yet
They simply can't deal with or move
on from the rain
They not quite ready for the sunny
days

Person five
Faces the rain
This person goes into the rain bare
naked walks up n hollers Bring It!
They have survived the rain
They have dealt with the rain
They know that in 5 minutes
The sunny days will be back
They understand the rain
And are willing to fight back
They have their rock or foundation
they have what they need to build
their house in any weather

They truly are one with the rain
They are the ones I wish to share
life with cuz I know that if we in
the rain together they got my back
n won't run cus of a little lighting n
thunder
They will defend me, shield me, love
me n will wait till they sun comes
out
N will say we good
Now let's have some fun…